Table of Contents

Introduction

Reading comprehension is vital for success in school and for success in many other areas of life. To become confident, independent readers, children need to read with understanding and make sense of new words. Young readers need practice to strengthen their reading comprehension abilities.

The **Head for Home Reading** series provides additional practice with reading comprehension skills for readers at all ability levels. The selections in each workbook cover a wide range of high-interest topics and include both fiction and nonfiction texts.

Head for Home Reading: Grade 3 Novice is designed to help struggling readers build and improve their reading comprehension. The Novice level for grade 3 includes eight lessons that target key reading skills. Each Novice lesson includes the following:

- An introduction defines the skill, explains why it is important, and provides step-by-step instructions for applying the skill.

- Guided Practice provides a reading selection with targeted, interactive reader-response questions that engage readers and build understanding of the skill.

- Independent Practice provides a reading selection, comprehension questions to check understanding, and a graphic organizer to reinforce the skill.

By choosing this workbook, you are helping your child build reading comprehension skills and achieve success in reading. A strong reading foundation will lead to a lifetime of reading enjoyment. Thank you for being involved in your child's learning. Here are a few suggestions for helping your child with reading comprehension.

- Read the instructions for each skill with your child. Preview the selection by looking at the title, images, and graphic organizer that follow.

- Help your child figure out the meaning of unfamiliar words through the context of the selection. Practice the new words with your child.

- Check the lesson when it is complete. Note areas of improvement and praise your child for success. Also note areas of concern and provide additional support as necessary.

Skill Focus: Characters

What are characters?

A **character** is a person or animal in a story. When you read a story, you learn about the characters by paying attention to what they do, say, think or feel.

Why are characters important?

The action of a story centers around the characters. Paying attention to what characters do, say, or think helps us better understand why characters act in certain ways to reach their goals. Understanding the actions of a character helps to bring meaning to a story.

How to Understand Characters:

▸ Read the story and identify the main characters. Ask yourself questions.

- *Who are the main characters? What do they look like?*

▸ Think about what the characters do during the story.

- *What actions do the characters take? Why do they act that way?*
- *How do the characters interact with one another? How do they treat others?*

▶ Think about what the characters say during the story.

   • *What do the characters talk about? Do their words match their actions?*

▶ Think about what the characters think or feel about what happens in the story.

   • *What do the characters think about the events in the story?*
   • *How do they feel about other characters? How do they feel about themselves?*

▶ You can write what a character does, says, and feels or thinks in a graphic organizer.

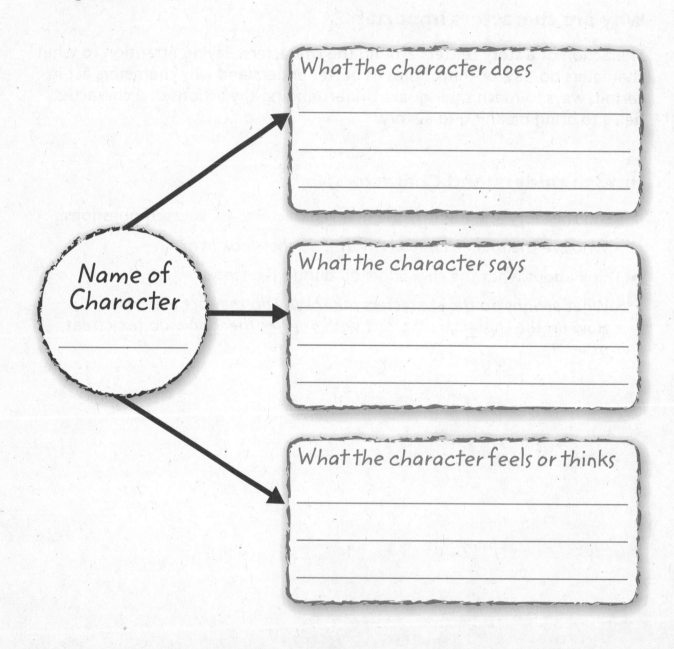

Directions: Read the story and answer the questions to learn more about characters.

Working Hard

Mia loved working on the computer at school. She enjoyed writing stories and drawing pictures to go with the stories. She liked solving math puzzles and problems.

1. Circle the main character's name.

One day Mia told her family that she wanted a computer. Her dad explained to her that it would cost a lot of money. So she showed him a page in the newspaper. A store was selling them at a special price. But her parents told her that it was still a lot of money.

"I'll earn the money myself," Mia said. "I'll work for our neighbors. I'll save all the money."

2. What do Mia's words tell you about her?

_____

_____

Mia's brother laughed at her idea. Alex told her she couldn't earn all that money. However, her parents said they would help her. They told her they would match the amount of money she earned each week. That meant if she earned five dollars in a week, they would give her five dollars. Mia was excited.

Mia began saving the money she earned by walking the neighbor's dog. She showed Alex the money she made in two weeks. He reminded her that she still needed a lot more money.

For many months, Mia found jobs working for other neighbors. She helped Mrs. Jones carry her bags of food from the store every week. She watched pets when people were away on trips. She took children to play at the park. She gathered soda cans and recycled them. Alex even helped her find soda cans.

3. Underline Mia's actions that help her reach her goal.

Finally, Mia thought she had enough money. Her family took her to the bank to get her money. Then they went to the store to look at the computers. The store had a surprise for Mia. The computer she wanted was on sale! She had more than enough money to buy it.

"I earned it," Mia said smiling.

"I didn't think you'd do it," Alex told her. "You really worked hard."

"Thank you," said Mia. "I'll let you play math games on the computer because you helped me!"

4. How do you think Mia feels at the end of the story?

_____

_____

_____

Directions: Read the story. Then answer the questions.

Camping

[1] Vanessa and Noura had planned to camp out in Noura's backyard for weeks. Now July had come and here they were. Noura's dad helped them decide where to make their camp. It was fun setting up their tent. They laughed as they struggled with the tent, tent poles, tent stakes, and ropes. Finally, the job was done. They unrolled their sleeping bags and placed them in the tent.

[2] Noura's dad looked over their camp and said it was the nicest camp he had ever seen. He told the girls he would see them in the morning, and then he went into the house. After the girls ate the sack lunches Vanessa's mother had made for them, they opened the book they had brought to read. Taking turns reading was fun, but soon they got tired. They turned off their flashlight, crawled into their sleeping bags, and went to sleep.

[3] Vanessa suddenly awoke and sat up feeling confused. "Where am I? Why is it so dark?" she wondered. She could just make out a bundled form next to her. Oh yes! Now she remembered. She was in a tent with her best friend, Noura.

[4] As Vanessa tried to go back to sleep, she heard a very strange sound. In a panic, she shook Noura awake.

[5] "What's wrong?" Noura asked.

[6] "I heard a strange sound, and I'm scared," Vanessa replied. "Listen."

[7] A short time later, the sound came again. "That's only an owl," whispered Noura. "Go back to sleep; it won't hurt us."

[8] "I wish I were inside the house!" cried Vanessa. "This is not fun anymore!"

[9] "If you really want to go inside, we can," Noura spoke quietly.

[10]"Yes, I'd like to very much," Vanessa said.

[11]The girls gathered their sleeping bags, opened the tent flap, walked to the back door of Noura's house, and went into the house. Vanessa thought inside was a very nice place to be.

Directions: Answer the questions.

1. Who are the two main characters in the story?

_____

_____

2. How do the characters feel in paragraphs 1–2?

_____

_____

3. How does Vanessa feel in paragraphs 3–4?

_____

_____

4. How does Noura react to Vanessa? Circle what she says to Vanessa.

_____

_____

5. How does Vanessa feel at the end of the story?

_____

_____

Directions: Choose one of the main characters. Use the graphic organizer to record information about what that character does, says, and feels or thinks.

Understanding Characters

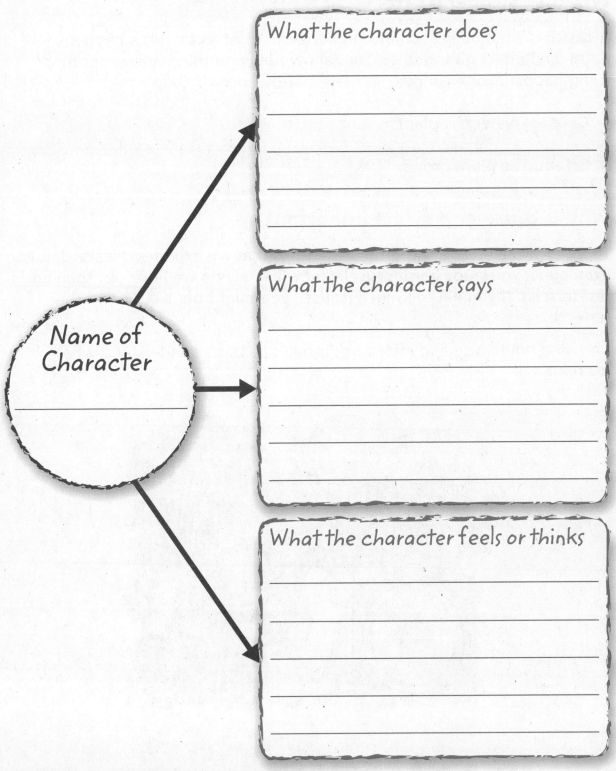

What the character does
_____
_____
_____
_____

Name of
Character
_____

What the character says
_____
_____
_____
_____

What the character feels or thinks
_____
_____
_____
_____

Skill Focus: Cause and Effect

What is cause and effect?

A **cause** is what makes something happen. An **effect** is what happens. Cause and effect go together. They show how one thing makes another thing happen. For example:

▸ **Cause:** I water the plant.

▸ **Effect:** The plant grows.

Why is cause and effect important?

There are many cause-and-effect situations that we experience each day. For example, if you study hard *(cause)*, you will likely do well on your spelling test *(effect)*. If you eat too much *(cause)*, you might get a stomachache *(effect)*.

Knowing how cause and effect works helps us better understand what we read.

How to Understand Cause and Effect:

▸ Read the story and identify what caused something to happen. Stop and ask yourself questions as you read.

- *Why did this happen?*
- *What was the cause?*

▸ Identify the effect, or what happened.

- *What happened?*
- *What was the effect?*

▸ You can write cause-and-effect sentences in a graphic organizer, like this.

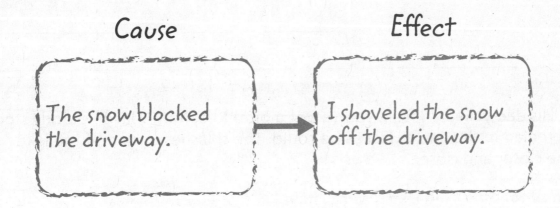

Cause   Effect

| The snow blocked the driveway. | → | I shoveled the snow off the driveway. |

Directions: Read the story and answer the questions to learn more about cause and effect.

Jacob's First Catch

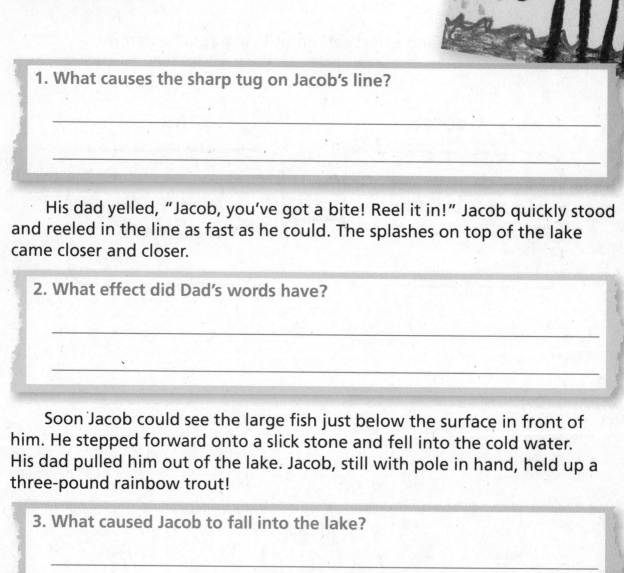

The morning was warming up. Just as Jacob was about to nap with his reel in hand, he felt a sharp tug. A fish was on his line! His pole bent toward the water.

1. What causes the sharp tug on Jacob's line?

_____

_____

His dad yelled, "Jacob, you've got a bite! Reel it in!" Jacob quickly stood and reeled in the line as fast as he could. The splashes on top of the lake came closer and closer.

2. What effect did Dad's words have?

_____

_____

Soon Jacob could see the large fish just below the surface in front of him. He stepped forward onto a slick stone and fell into the cold water. His dad pulled him out of the lake. Jacob, still with pole in hand, held up a three-pound rainbow trout!

3. What caused Jacob to fall into the lake?

_____

_____

Sofia's Treasure

Sofia always wore the necklace. She loved the beads with the beautiful purple heart! She had found it at the beach. Sofia and her mom had tried to find the owner. Sofia thought a princess must have lost it long ago.

4. Why did Sofia always wear the necklace?

_____

_____

One evening Sofia sat down to eat dinner. Her mom gasped. "Sofia, where is your necklace?" Sofia quickly felt from her chin to her collar. The necklace was gone. They searched. They could not find it. Sofia cried herself to sleep.

5. What happened when Sofia's mom saw the necklace was missing?

_____

_____

The next morning, Sofia stayed in her bed. Her mom walked in with the necklace. She said, "Look what I found. It was caught inside the sweater you wore yesterday." Sofia sprung off her bed. She hugged her mother tightly.

6. What happened when Sofia's mom found the necklace?

_____

_____

Directions: Read the story and answer the questions. Then, reread the story. Underline at least one cause, and circle its effect.

Mrs. Feather's Special Treat

[1] The children in Mrs. Feather's class were all lined up outside the classroom. "I have a special treat for you boys and girls," she said. "The eggs in the classroom have finally hatched!" The children all screamed.

[2] Hugo jumped up and down three times. But the third time, he stepped on Maria's big toe. Maria left to see the nurse.

[3] Sal lifted his lunchbox into the air and said, "Yes!" His juice box fell out. Juice spilled on the ground. He had to go tell Mr. James, the custodian.

[4] Tina became afraid. She started to cry. She said that she was scared of creatures. Mrs. Feather sent her to the office to call her mom.

[5] However, the most excitement happened when Mrs. Feather opened the door. Two chicks ran out into the hallway. Three more had made a mess on her desk.

[6] Lee laughed. "You're right, Mrs. Feather. This is a special treat!"

Directions: Answer the questions.

1. What caused the children to scream?

A. Sal's juice box fell out of his lunchbox, spilling juice on the ground.

B. Two chicks ran out into the hallway.

C. Mrs. Feather told the class that the chicks had hatched.

2. What happened after Hugo jumped up and down and stepped on Maria's toe?

A. He scared Tina and she started to cry.

B. Maria left to see the nurse.

C. The children started to scream.

3. Why did the chicks run out the doorway?

A. Mrs. Feather opened the door.

B. The screaming children frightened them.

C. Lee laughed.

4. Why was Mrs. Feather excited?

A. The eggs had hatched.

B. The children were lined up quietly.

C. The class was studying animals.

Directions: Use the graphic organizer to record the causes and effects in the story.

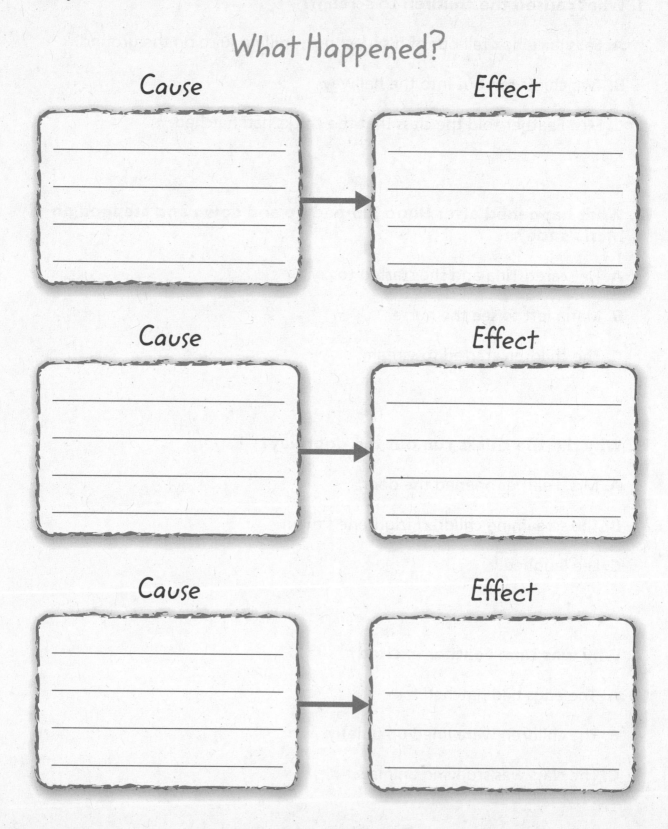

What Happened?

Cause

Effect

Cause

Effect

Cause

Effect

Skill Focus: Main Idea and Details

What is a main idea? What is a detail?

The **main idea** tells what a selection is mostly about. **Details** give more information about the main idea. The main idea of a selection is usually found at the beginning.

Suppose you read a selection about pets, such as dogs. When you read it, you learn how to care for a dog's needs, such as what to feed it, how to groom it, and how to keep it healthy. The main idea of the selection is: *A pet dog has many needs*. One detail might be: *Wash your dog to keep it groomed*.

Why are main ideas and details important?

When we identify a selection's main idea and describe details that tell more about it, we show that we understand what we read.

How to Understand Main Ideas and Details:

▸ Read the selection. Think about and decide what the selection is about. Ask yourself questions.

  • *What is the selection mostly about?*
  • *How would I describe the main idea?*

▶ Think about and decide what information tells more about the main idea.

- *What is a detail that gives me more information?*
- *What details can I find in the selection that tell me more about the main idea?*

▶ You can write the selection's main idea and details in a graphic organizer, like this one.

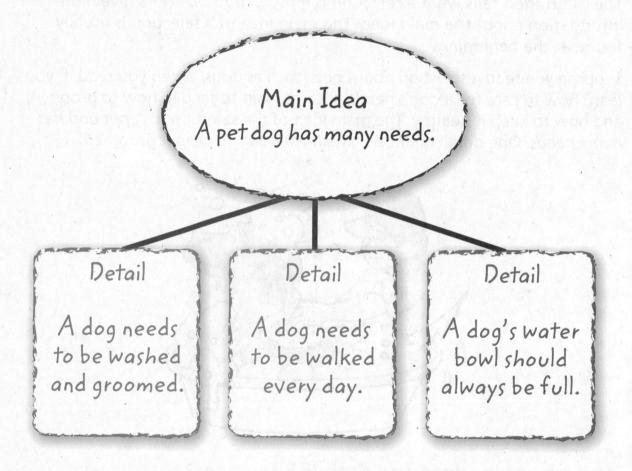

Main Idea
A pet dog has many needs.

Detail

A dog needs to be washed and groomed.

Detail

A dog needs to be walked every day.

Detail

A dog's water bowl should always be full.

Directions: Read the selection and answer the questions to learn more about main idea and details.

Stars and Stripes Forever

There are many symbols of our country. The United States flag is one of them. It has been flying high for over 225 years.

The United States flag is the third oldest flag in the world. It is older than the flags of England and France. The United States flag was first made official on June 14, 1777. Every year on this date, Flag Day is observed in the United States.

When the flag was first made, it was ordered that a star and a stripe be shown for each colony. At that time the United States had only 13 colonies. This meant that the flag had 13 stars. It also had 13 stripes. Today, the flag still has 13 stripes. But it has 50 stars: one for each state in the United States.

1. Circle two details that tell about the flag today.

The colors on the flag also have meaning. The red stands for courage. The white stands for hope. The blue stands for truth.

> **2. Circle three details that tell about the colors on the flag.**

Each star represents a state. The stars stand for power and control. This means each state is free within the United States.

> **3. What do the stars on the flag stand for?**
>
> _____
>
> _____

George Washington said this about the American flag:
We take the stars from Heaven, the red from our mother country, separating it by white stripes, thus showing that we have separated from her, and the white stripes shall go down to posterity representing Liberty.

The American flag is here to stay. It will always fly high as long as we are "one nation under God with liberty and justice for all."

> **4. What is the main idea of this selection?**
>
> _____
>
> _____
>
> _____

The National Symbol

[1] Have you ever seen the image of a bald eagle on the back of a coin? Its wings are spread, showing its glory. The bald eagle is the national symbol of the United States. It was chosen because of its long life, great strength, and majestic look. Back then, it was thought to live only in North America.

[2] The bald eagle lives in high mountains and steep cliffs. It has unlimited choice of where it will fly. It may fly high in the sky. It may soar low along the valleys. Freedom is what it has. Freedom is what it stands for.

[3] There are many stories about how the bald eagle became a symbol of the United States. During the Revolutionary War, the noise of the fighting awoke the eagles. They flew in circles above the fighting men. This led one of the soldiers to say the eagles were "shrieking for freedom."

[4] The bald eagle became a national symbol on June 20, 1782. This is when the Great Seal of the United States was adopted. The Great Seal shows an eagle with its wings spread. It is facing forward and has a shield with 13 red and white stripes on its chest. Above the eagle is a blue field with 13 stars. The eagle holds an olive branch in its right talon. In its left talon, it holds 13 arrows. There is a scroll in its beak. It reads "*E Pluribus Unum.*" This is the motto of the United States. It means "one out of many."

⁵The bald eagle was almost not the national symbol of the United States. Ben Franklin did not like the bald eagle. He wanted the turkey to be the symbol. He said, "The turkey is a much more respectable bird. . . ." Thank goodness Mr. Franklin did not get his wish. Try to think of a turkey being the symbol of our country!

Directions: Answer the questions.

1. What is the main idea of this selection?

_____

_____

_____

_____

_____

2. Circle the sentence in paragraph 1 that tell reasons why the bald eagle was chosen as our national symbol.

3. Circle two sentences in paragraph 2 that give details about what life is like for a bald eagle living in the wild.

4. What three details in paragraph 4 tell more about the Great Seal?

_____

_____

_____

_____

Directions: Use the graphic organizer to record the selection's main idea and details.

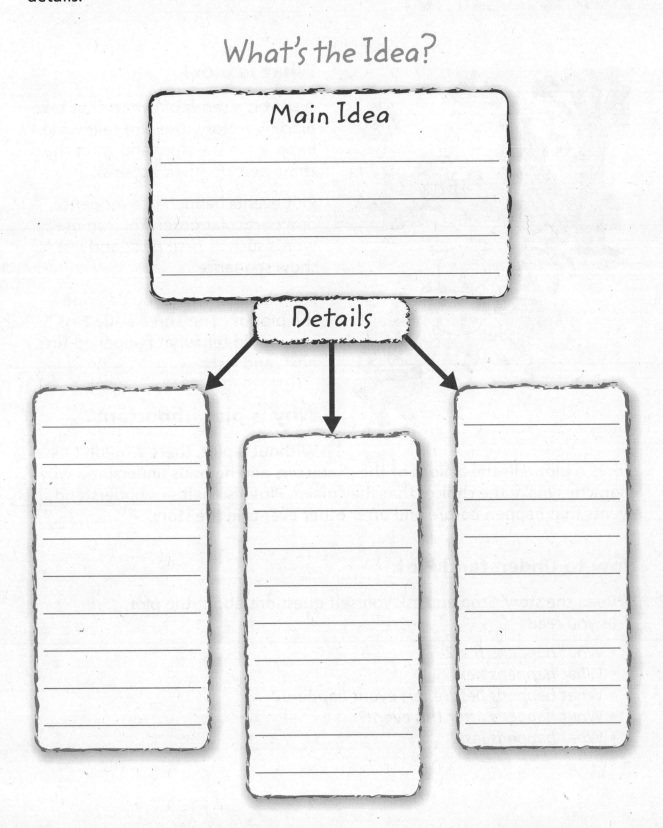

What's the Idea?

Main Idea

Details

Main Idea and Details
Head for Home Reading, Grade 3

Skill Focus: Plot

What is plot?

A **plot** is a series of events that take place in a story. The plot tells what happens in the story and what the characters do (their actions).

Plot events happen in a sequence, or a particular order. You can use words such as *first, next,* and *last* to show sequence.

For example, when you describe the plot of "The Three Little Pigs," you would tell what happened first, next, and last.

Why is plot important?

Without a plot, there wouldn't be a story! A plot tells the actions of the characters and helps us understand why characters make the choices that they make. Plot also helps us understand events that happen *before* and *after* other events in the story.

How to Understand Plot:

▸ Read the story. Stop and ask yourself questions about the plot as you read.

- *What happens first?*
- *What happens next?*
- *What happens before this event happens?*
- *What happens after this event?*
- *What happens last?*

▸ Identify the main events that happen in the story.

▸ You can write the order of the main events in a graphic organizer. Use transition words such as *first, next, before, after, but, so,* and *last* to tell about the events.

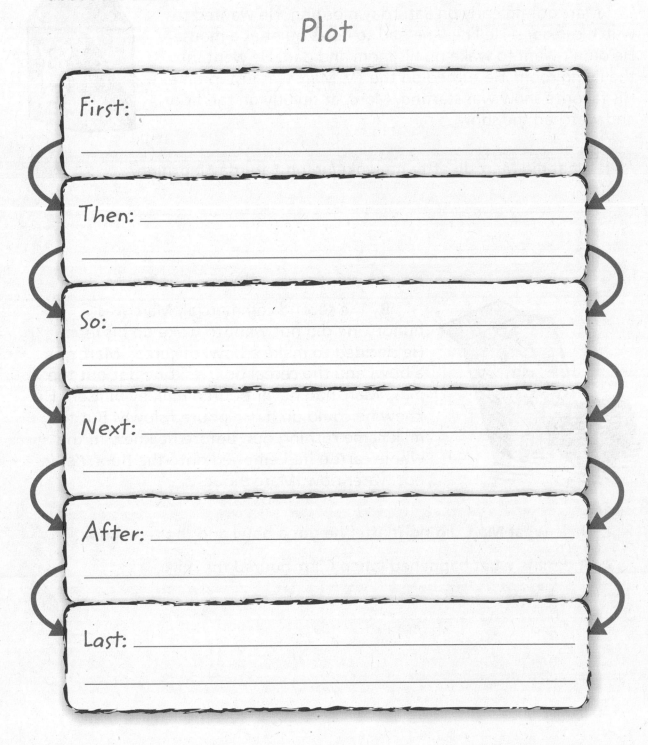

Plot

First: _____

_____

Then: _____

_____

So: _____

_____

Next: _____

_____

After: _____

_____

Last: _____

_____

Directions: Read the story and answer the questions to learn more about plot.

What a Mess!

Marc got up early on Saturday morning. He wanted to watch cartoons. He knew he had to be as quiet as a mouse. He didn't want to wake up his mom and dad. He went into the living room. He turned on the TV. Marc was just in time. His favorite show was starting. Marc sat quietly on the floor and watched the show.

1. What did Marc do after he woke up on Saturday morning?

_____

_____

By the second commercial, Marc was hungry. He did not want to wake up his mom. He decided to make a bowl of cereal. Marc got a bowl and the cereal box. Next he got out the milk. Marc had never poured milk by himself. He knew he could do it. He poured slowly. But the milk came rushing out. Before he knew it, the whole carton had emptied onto the floor. *I'm in hot water now*, Marc thought.

2. Circle what Marc did right after he got a bowl and the cereal box.

3. Underline what happened when Marc poured the milk.

Milk was all over the floor. Marc found a roll of paper towels and began to wipe up the mess. His mom walked in. She was very upset.

"What are you doing?" she asked.

4. What did Marc do to clean up the milk on the floor?

_____

_____

_____

_____

Marc said that he was trying to make breakfast without waking her. Then he said that the milk carton just tipped over. All the milk had spilled out. His mom started to laugh. She said it was okay and helped him clean up the mess. After the mess was cleaned up, his mom suggested they go to get a breakfast treat and more milk. Marc's stomach growled. He thought that was a great idea.

5. Underline what happened after Marc's mom laughed.

6. What did Marc and his mom do at the end of the story?

_____

_____

_____

_____

Plot
Head for Home Reading, Grade 3

Directions: Read the story and answer the questions to learn more about plot.

Going to the State Fair

[1]Teva had been waiting for the state fair to begin. She loved going to the fair to have fun on the rides and eat popcorn, but most of all she loved to spend time at the animal shows.

[2]Teva and her mom walked out to the car. "Don't forget the snacks," said Teva. It was a long drive to the state fair, and Mom had decided to take some fruit, vegetable sticks, and crackers along so they would only have to stop for gas.

[3]"Everything is loaded," said Mom. "It looks as if we can go now." Mom turned the key. The car made a clicking sound and wouldn't start. She kept trying, but it was no use. "I think we may have a dead battery," said Mom.

[4]"But, Mom, what about the state fair?" cried Teva. She had looked forward to going to the fair for weeks.

[5]"I'm sorry, Teva. I don't think we'll be able to go. I'll have to call a tow truck and get the car to a repair station," said Mom.

[6]They both got out of the car. Mom went into the living room and picked up the telephone. Teva took all the snacks back into the kitchen and began putting them away.

[7]A few minutes later, she heard a horn honking on the street. She ran outside to see what was going on. She saw her grandpa's red truck. "Grandpa, what are you doing here?" asked Teva.

[8]"Well, I thought you might need a ride to the state fair," said Grandpa.

[9]"How did you know our car wouldn't start?" asked Teva.

[10]"Your mom called me, of course!" said Grandpa with a twinkle in his eyes.

[11]"I'll go get the snacks!" said Teva breathlessly. She ran into the house. Her sadness was gone. Now that Grandpa was going with them to the state fair, she was even more excited about going. After loading Grandpa's truck, the three of them headed to the state fair.

[12]Grandpa, Mom, and Teva rode on rides, ate popcorn, and spent time petting all the animals.

[13]"Thank you for saving the day, Grandpa," said Teva. The three smiled as they walked out to the truck to drive home.

Directions: Answer the questions.

1. What happens first in the story?

_____

_____

_____

2. What happens when Mom and Teva get in the car?

_____

_____

_____

3. What happens next?

_____

_____

4. What happens after Teva puts the snacks away?

_____

_____

5. What happens at the end of the story?

_____

_____

Directions: Read the story again. Use the graphic organizer to record the plot's events.

Describe the Plot

First: _____
_____
_____

Then: _____
_____
_____

So: _____
_____
_____

Next: _____
_____
_____

After: _____
_____
_____

Last: _____
_____
_____

Skill Focus: Problem and Resolution

What is a problem? What is a resolution?

In a story, a **problem** is something difficult that a character has to deal with. A **resolution** is how a character solves, or works out, the problem.

Think about a problem that you deal with in school. Suppose you and some friends want to play with the same toy. How would you solve the problem? Do you work it out by taking turns? Or do you find a way to play with the toy at the same time?

Why is resolving a problem important?

Identifying a problem and how it is resolved helps us better understand what the characters are going through in a story. Learning how to solve problems is also a valuable skill that can help us in our everyday lives.

How to Understand a Problem and a Resolution:

▸ Read the story. As you read, ask yourself questions.

- *Who is the main character?*
- *What problem is this character dealing with in the story?*
- *How does the character feel about the problem?*

▸ Think about how the character works out the problem.

　• *What steps does the character take to try and resolve the problem?*
　• *How is the problem solved at the end of the story?*

▸ You can write the problem and its resolution in a graphic organizer, like this one.

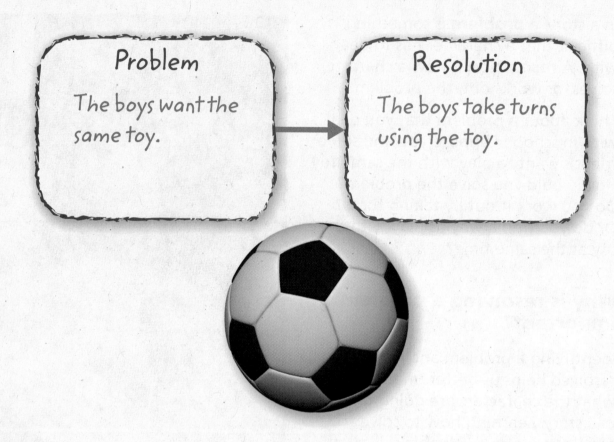

Problem

The boys want the same toy.

Resolution

The boys take turns using the toy.

Directions: Read the story and answer the questions to learn more about solving problems.

It's Gone

Lalya looked all around. She thought she remembered putting her homework next to her backpack. But it was not there; it was gone.

1. Underline the name of the main character.

2. What is the main character's problem?

_____

_____

She looked in her bedroom. It was not there. She looked in the kitchen. It was not there either. She looked and looked in every nook and cranny around the house. Her homework was nowhere to be found. What was she going to do?

3. What did the character do to solve her problem?

_____

_____

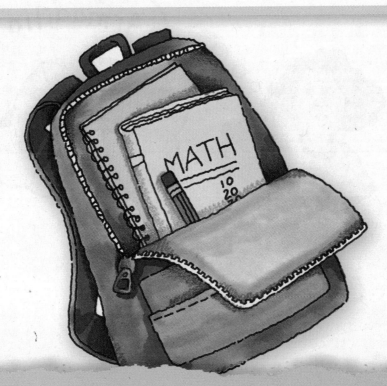

Problem and Resolution
Head for Home Reading, Grade 3

She thought about going to school without her homework, but that would not be good. Doing her homework was important. She always did her homework and had never turned it in late. She had never in her short time in school not done her homework. She was not going to start now.

4. Circle one idea the character has to solve the problem.

5. Why did the character decide not to do this?

_____

_____

She still had about thirty minutes until she had to catch the bus. So she decided to redo it. Thank goodness she could remember her spelling words. Now she could look up the definitions again and write the sentences. Then her homework redo would be done.

6. How did the character solve her problem?

_____

_____

Directions: Read the story and answer the questions.

Good Deed

[1] It was a chilly fall day. Frost covered the windowpanes on the log cabin home. Alonso and his family lived on the edge of a forest. There was a hint of winter in the air. Alonso could smell it. His mom had asked him to gather branches to build a fire. So he put on his sweatshirt and gloves and headed outside.

[2] Alonso began picking up branches under the nearby trees and breaking them into smaller pieces. He thought he heard something. So he stopped. He didn't hear anything. Then he started breaking the branches again and thought he heard the same noise. He stopped and listened—nothing. Just as he was about to pick up the pile, he heard it. A faint chorus of whimpering was coming from a nearby bush.

[3] Alonso silently crept over to the bush. When he looked into the bush, he thought he saw something move. So he reached his hands into the bush and separated the leaves and twigs. There tucked inside the bush were a dog and her puppies. The dog was as skinny as could be. She must have been abandoned. *She and the pups must be starving*, Alonso thought. *What should I do?*

[4] Alonso knew he couldn't let the dog starve. He headed back toward the house. Then he silently opened the back door and tiptoed into the kitchen. He opened the refrigerator and found a pot of leftover chicken.

Thank goodness his mom was folding laundry in the bedroom. She would be angry when she found it was gone. The family was going to have it for lunch. Then he went to get a couple of bowls from the cupboard. All that was there was his mother's good china. He could not use that. "What am I going to put the food and water in?" he whispered to himself. "I know!"

Problem and Resolution
Head for Home Reading, Grade 3

[5]Alonso quietly raced to his room and grabbed two small tubs filled with toys. He dumped the toys on the floor and ran back to the kitchen. He filled one bowl with water and the other with chicken.

[6]When the dog noticed Alonso with the food, her ears perked up. She ate and drank like she hadn't had food in days. About an hour later, the pups were busy nursing. Now they would not be hungry.

[7]When Alonso's mom found out what he had done, she was not mad. She was proud of him. He had seen someone in need and was responsible enough to help.

Directions: Answer the questions.

1. Who is the main character?

A. the starving dog

B. Alonso

C. Alonso's mom

2. What is the problem?

A. Alonso was too young to chop wood.

B. It was almost too cold to gather branches for a fire.

C. Alonso discovered a starving dog and her pups.

3. What is the resolution to the problem?

A. Alonso found food and water for the dogs.

B. Alonso asked his parents to feed the dogs.

C. Alonso called animal control about the dogs.

Directions: Use the graphic organizer to record information about a problem and its resolution.

Problem and Resolution

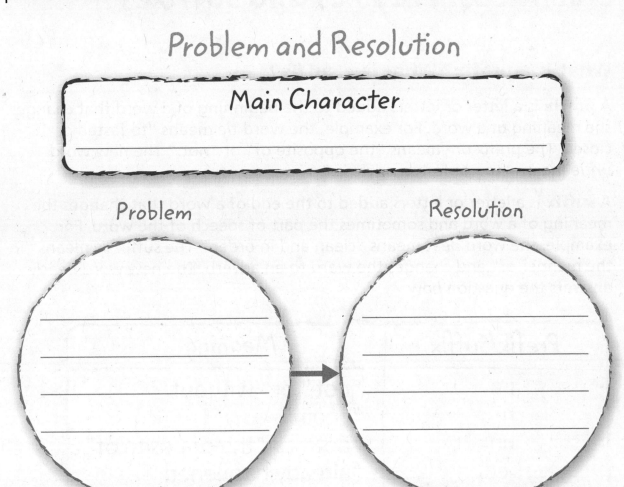

Main Character

_____

Problem

Resolution

Skill Focus: Prefixes and Suffixes

What is a prefix? What is a suffix?

A **prefix** is a letter or letters added to the beginning of a word that changes the meaning of a word. For example, the word *tie* means "to fasten or close." The prefix *un-* means "the opposite of" or "not." The new word *untie* means "to not fasten or close."

A **suffix** is a letter or letters added to the end of a word that changes the meaning of a word and sometimes the part of speech of the word. For example, the word *neat* means "clean and in order." The suffix *-ly* means "in the manner of" and changes the word to an adverb. The new word *neatly* answers the question *how*.

Prefix/Suffix	Meaning
im-	"not" or "without"
re-	"again"
un-	"not" or "the opposite of"
-ed	"already happened"
-est	"the most"
-ing	"in the process of"
-less	"not having" or "without"
-ly	"in the manner of"

Why are prefixes and suffixes important?

Knowing the meaning of the prefix or suffix of a word helps us understand the meaning of a word. Knowing how a prefix or suffix can change a word's part of speech helps us to identify how the word is used in a sentence.

How to Understand Prefixes and Suffixes:

▸ Identify words that have a prefix, such as *un-, pre-, mis- re-, pro-*. Ask yourself questions.

 • *What is the meaning of the word without the prefix?*
 • *What is the meaning of the word with the prefix?*

▸ Identify words that have a suffix, such as *-ly, -ed, -er, -est,* and *-ing*. Then, ask similar questions as those above.

▸ You can write words with prefixes or suffixes in a graphic organizer. Circle the prefix or suffix, then analyze the word's meaning, like this.

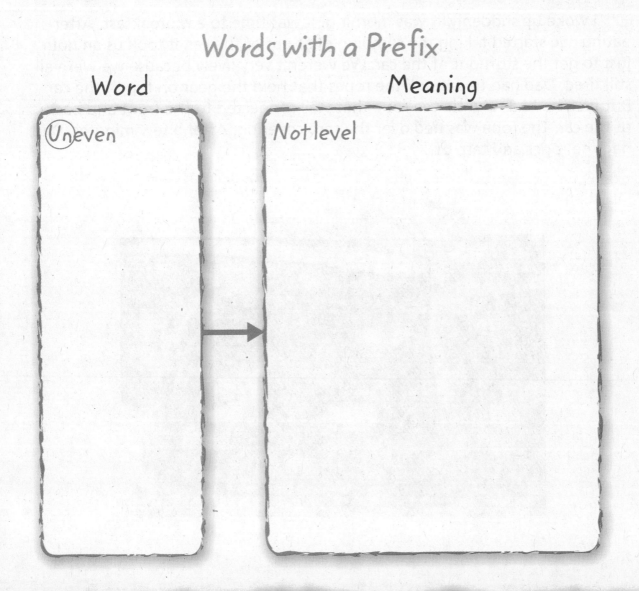

Words with a Prefix

Word

Meaning

(Un)even

Not level

Prefixes and Suffixes
Head for Home Reading, Grade 3

Directions: Read the story and answer the questions to learn more about prefixes and suffixes.

Unpacking After a Camping Trip

Our week's camping vacation went by quickly. But the unpacking took what seemed like years. We had arrived home late. Dad said that we would not unload the gear until morning. Dad parked the car in the garage. We slowly walked upstairs and fell into our beds. We slept silently until morning.

1. Underline words with the prefix *un-*.

2. Circle words with the suffix *-ly*.

I woke up suddenly. It was morning. It was time to eat breakfast. After eating, we started taking the camping gear out of the car. It took us an hour just to get the stuff out of the car. We weren't very lively because we were all still tired. Dad had to unhook the ropes that held the gear on top of the car. But first, he had to untie the rope that was connected to the front and back of the car. The rope was tied over the tarp covering. After a few minutes, Dad had the ropes and tarp off.

The gear was uncovered. We began lifting the gear carefully off the roof of the car. Everything was finally off the top and out of the inside of the car. It all was lying on the front lawn in an disorganized way.

3. Underline words with prefix *un-*. Write a new sentence using one of the words.

_____

_____

_____

_____

Now it was time to unroll and unzip the sleeping bags so they could air out. Mom hung them on the clothesline in the backyard. All the sleeping bags smelled bad.

After a few hours we were finished. Then we ate lunch and took a long nap.

4. What two words with prefixes describe what the family did with the sleeping bags?

_____

_____

5. Circle words with the suffix *-ed*.

Directions: Read the story and answer the questions. Then, read the passage again. Circle words with prefixes. Underline words with suffixes.

A Terrible Dream

[1]When I went to bed last night, I found that it was impossible to fall asleep. I became restless and tossed and turned. When I finally fell asleep, I had the scariest dream ever.

[2]I dreamt that I was in bed (which I was!) and I heard an unusual noise. It sounded as if someone were shuffling his feet along the floor. When I opened my eyes, I saw something unbelievable. A spooky-looking creature was moving toward my bed. It was bigger than anything I'd ever seen. I began to shake all over. When I tried to get up and run, I was unable to move. As the monster was about to grab my hand, I made myself wake up.

[3]It's useless to think that I'll forget this dream. So maybe I'll retell the dream to my friends at school tomorrow, just to give them something to think about! In the meantime, I'm looking forward to a restful sleep—and sweet dreams tonight!

Directions: Answer the questions.

1. **Which word has a prefix?**

   A. impossible

   B. scariest

   C. bigger

2. **Which word means "without quiet and ease"?**

   A. rest

   B. restful

   C. restless

3. **Which word does NOT have a suffix?**

   A. unusual

   B. useless

   C. shuffling

4. **Which word has a prefix?**

   A. believe

   B. unbelievable

   C. believable

Directions: Use the graphic organizer to sort and record words with prefixes and suffixes. Then write each word's meaning. If necessary, use a dictionary to check the meaning of words.

Words with Prefixes and Suffixes

Words with a Prefix

Word   Meaning

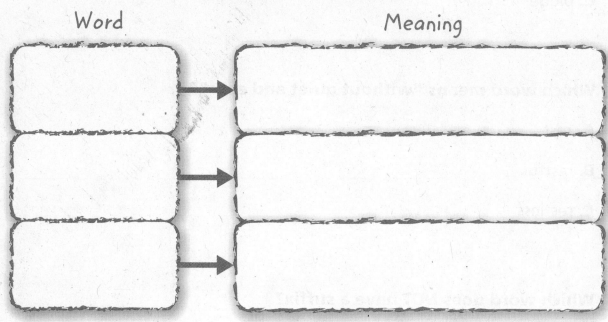

Words with a Suffix

Word   Meaning

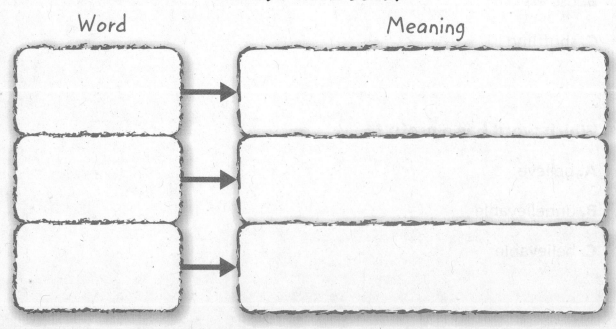

Skill Focus: Author's Purpose

What is an author's purpose?

An author writes for many reasons. These reasons are called an **author's purpose.**

Sometimes authors try to **persuade,** or convince readers to do something or to think a certain way. For example: *A dog is the best pet. A dog will protect you and is a loyal friend. You should go to an animal shelter and get a dog!*

When an author gives the reader facts, the author is trying to **inform** the reader. For example: *The Old English sheepdog is a large dog. It has two layers of thick fur.*

Other authors may want to tell a story or write about something that readers will enjoy reading. In this case, the author's purpose is to **entertain**. For example: *Spot rushed into the closet and changed. He came out as "Super Dog," the defender of the helpless!*

Why is an author's purpose important?

Identifying the author's purpose helps us understand the message the author wants us to get from his or her writing.

Author's Purpose
Head for Home Reading, Grade 3

How to Understand an Author's Purpose:

▸ Read the selection. Then ask yourself questions.

- *Did the author write it to persuade, or convince me to do something or to think a certain way?*
- *Did the author write it to inform, or give me facts and important information about a topic?*
- *Did the author write it to entertain, or have me enjoy reading the selection?*

▸ Highlight or take notes about details that support the author's purpose. Then tell whether the author's purpose was to persuade, inform, or entertain.

▸ You can write the author's purpose in a graphic organizer, like this one. Identify the author's purpose. Write evidence, or details, that support the purpose.

Author's Purpose	Evidence
_____	_____
_____	_____
_____	_____

Directions: Read the following selections and answer the questions to learn more about an author's purpose.

Your Eating Habits

Having healthy eating habits is important. When you eat healthy foods, you have more energy, sleep better, and get sick less often. If you eat too much fast food and not enough good food, you won't have as much energy. Eating healthy foods keeps your immune system healthy. This system fights off infections. If it isn't strong enough, you can get sick.

1. **What is the author's message?**

_____

_____

_____

Eating a well-balanced diet includes eating whole-grain bread, cereal, pasta, and rice. It also includes eating lots of fruits and veggies. Low-fat milk and yogurt are good for you too. Lean meats, such as turkey and chicken, as well as fish and nuts are good choices at dinnertime. So eat healthy foods because your body will thank you!

2. **Did the author write this selection to inform or to entertain readers? How do you know?**

_____

_____

_____

Park or Mini-mall: You Decide

There is a park in our neighborhood. It is filled with trees and has a playground. There are walking trails and even a basketball court. There are always people in the park. You see families with their children and couples walking hand in hand. You see people walking their dogs and kids playing basketball. When you look around the park, you see happy people.

4. How does the author feel about the park? How do you know?

_____

_____

_____

However, this may soon come to an end. Builders want to build a mini-mall where the park is. They say that the people in the neighborhood would rather have stores nearby. They say that the kids would love to go to the mall to see all the new toys. They say that it would be a great place for families to go. But we don't need more stores. We need our park.

5. Underline how the author feels about a park versus a mini-mall.

We already have a large mall three miles away. The only other park in our city is ten miles away. It doesn't have a playground or walking trails. This is our neighborhood park. It is a clean and safe place to go to enjoy the outdoors.

The city is letting the people decide. There is a town meeting on Monday.

Mark your calendar! Every vote counts! Save our park!

6. What is the author's purpose for writing this selection?

_____

The Letter

1 January 21, 2012

2 Dear Mayor,

3 I would like to tell you about something important. Each day that I walk to school I have to cross First Street. The cars go by very fast. Sometimes the drivers in the cars do not pay attention to the crossing guard. I am afraid that someone will get hurt one day. Could you please put a stoplight on First Street near Grant School? It sure would make getting to school much safer.

4 Yours truly,

5 Luke Smyth

Student

Directions: Answer the questions.

1. Why is Luke writing to the mayor?

A. He is writing a report on community safety and wants to inform the mayor about a problem.

B. He wants more crossing guards to work near school because drivers are speeding.

C. He wants a stoplight installed near the school because drivers are ignoring the crossing guard.

2. Luke's purpose for writing the letter is to

A. inform

B. persuade

C. entertain

3. Which of the following sentences shows Luke's feelings?

A. It sure would make getting to school much safer.

B. Each day that I walk to school I have to cross First Street.

C. The cars go by very fast.

Directions: Use the graphic organizer to record information about the author's purpose.

Identifying Author's Purpose

Author's Purpose	Evidence

Skill Focus: Setting

What is setting?

A **setting** tells *where* and *when* a story takes place. The setting is where and when the action of a story happens. A story can have more than one setting.

For example, think about the setting of "Little Red Riding Hood." When does the story take place? *(one morning)* Where does the story take place? *(in the woods)* Does the setting change in the story? *(Little Red Riding Hood goes to her grandmother's house in the woods.)*

Why is setting important?

A setting is important to a story's meaning because it tells where and when all of the action in a story take place. Knowing where and when a story takes places helps us more fully understand what is happening in a story.

How to Understand Setting:

▸ Read the story. Stop and ask yourself questions about the setting as you read.

- *Where does the story take place?*
- *Does the setting change during the story?*

▸ Circle words or phrases that tell where the story takes place.

- *When does the story happen?*

▸ Underline words or phrases that tell when the story takes place.

- *How does the setting set up the action in the story?*
- *Why is the setting important to this story's meaning?*

▸ You can write information about the setting in a graphic organizer, like this one.

Where does it happen?

_____

_____

When does it happen?

_____

_____

Directions: Read the selection and answer the questions to learn more about setting.

A Hike to Remember

I can still remember all the days I spent with my father. When I was nine, my father and I began hiking in the mountains around our house. We would go hiking once or twice a month on the weekends. I can clearly recall the first time we went hiking together. I still remember it as if it were just yesterday.

It was a Saturday morning. It was a beautiful spring day. We spent the early hours of the morning packing our gear. We each packed sunscreen, a first-aid kit, a compass, water, and food into a backpack. It was chilly as the sun was just starting to peek through the trees by our house. I was chilly, so I put on my jacket.

1. Circle where the story takes place.

2. Underline when the story takes place.

After we had eaten breakfast, we jumped in the car. We drove about twenty miles to the trailhead of the Lost Dutchman Trail. My dad had told me how beautiful the views from this trail were. So it was the clear choice for our first hike together.

Once the sun was up, the temperature began to rise. It was starting to get warm as we started our hike. The beginning of the trail was pretty flat. But soon the trail got steeper. After we had been walking for a while, we came around some rocks and saw the real trail. It seemed as if it was almost straight up. I looked at it, thinking that I could never climb that. But my father sensed my fear. He laughed and pointed in the other direction. "We're going that way," he said, and chuckled.

When I turned to look at the other trail, I saw that it was not as steep. That was more like it. I needed something easy for our first hike.

After hiking for about ten minutes, my father stopped. I was so busy looking around that I ran right into him. He turned around. "Shhhhh, listen," he whispered.

I could hear a rumbling sound that was growing louder. Then it stopped.

"Sounded like a small landslide," my father said. "But it's over now."

"You're not worried about it?" I said.

"Nah," he replied. "It didn't sound that bad." And we kept going.

But after about a hundred feet we came upon the source of the sound. Rocks had fallen down the side of the rock wall. They had completely blocked the trail.

3. Underline the event that causes a problem.

My father let out a sigh. "Well," he said, "I guess we're not going this way. We'll have to turn around and use the other trail."

"You're kidding," I commented. "Up that steep trail?"

"Yeah," he replied. "It is not that bad. You'll be able to handle it."

He didn't seem worried, so I wasn't worried. "Remind me to call the park rangers when we get back to let them know about the landslide."

My father was right. I didn't have any trouble climbing the other trail. It was actually really fun. This was just the first of many hiking adventures I had with my father. I miss those days!

4. How does the mountain setting affect the action in the story?

_____

_____

_____

Setting
Head for Home Reading, Grade 3

A Night Show

[1]Oscar quickly finished his dinner. It was already getting dark. He wanted to go outside with his parents to look at the stars. It was the end of March, so it was the perfect time of year. It got dark at the perfect time—not too early, not too late. They put all the dishes away. Then they headed outside with a bunch of blankets.

[2]They turned off the backyard lights so it would be even darker. They lay down in the middle of the grass. They chose a spot far from the pine trees so they wouldn't be poked by their needles. The weather was cold, but the grass was dry and smooth. Oscar squeezed between his parents, and they bundled up with their blankets to be warm and cozy. The scene in front of them was amazing! The sky seemed to have its own blanket of stars.

[3]It was quiet, so they heard the noises of the night in the background. The wind blew through the trees, making the limbs creak. The crickets filled the night with music. Oscar had looked at the stars so many times. He already knew the names of the different constellations. He also liked to stare at the sky and wait to see if he could catch a shooting star. Oscar couldn't think of a better thing to do before going to bed.

Directions: Answer the questions.

1. When does the story happen?

_____

_____

_____

2. Where does the story happen?

_____

_____

_____

3. What is the action in the story?

_____

_____

_____

4. How does the setting of the story affect the action?

_____

_____

_____

Directions: Use the graphic organizer to record information about the story's setting.

Setting the Stage

Where does it happen?

_____

_____

_____

_____

_____

When does it happen?

_____

_____

_____

_____

_____

Answer Key

Characters, pp. 3–9

Guided Practice: Working Hard, pp. 5–6

1. Circle: Mia

2. Possible answer: The computer is important to her. She is a hard worker and will earn money for the computer.

3. Underline: Mia began saving the money she earned by walking the neighbor's dog. She helped Mrs. Jones carry her bags of food from the store every week. She watched pets when people were away on trips. She took children to play at the park. She gathered soda cans and recycled them.

4. Possible answer: She feels proud of herself and happy to have worked hard to earn a computer.

Independent Practice: Camping, pp. 7–8

1. Noura and Vanessa

2. They are happy and having fun.

3. At first, she is confused. Then, she is scared.

4. Noura tries to calm her down.
Circle: "That's only an owl," "Go back to sleep; it won't hurt us." "If you really want to go inside, we can."

5. She feels safe and happy in the house.

Graphic Organizer: Understanding Characters, p. 9

Possible answer:

Name of character: Vanessa

What she does: Sets up tent, goes to sleep, wakes up, gets scared, wakes Noura up

What she says: "I heard a strange sound, and I'm scared." "I wish I were inside the house!" "This is not fun anymore!"

What she feels or thinks: She is happy to camp at the beginning. She gets scared by the strange sounds. She feels better inside the house.

Cause and Effect, pp. 10–16

Guided Practice: Jacob's First Catch, p. 12

1. A fish is on the line.
2. Jacob stood and reeled in the line as fast as he could.
3. Jacob stepped onto a slick stone.

Guided Practice: Sofia's Treasure, p. 13

1. Sofia loved the necklace.
2. Sofia and her mom searched for the necklace.
3. Sofia jumped off the bed and hugged her mother.

Independent Practice: Mrs. Feather's Special Treat, pp. 14–15

1. C
2. B
3. A
4. A

Graphic Organizer: What Happened? p. 16

Possible answers:

Cause: Hugo jumped up and down and stepped on Maria's toe.
Effect: Maria left to see the nurse.

Cause: Sal lifted his lunchbox into the air and his juice box fell out.
Effect: Juice spilled on the ground and Sal went to get the custodian.

Cause: Tina was scared of creatures.
Effect: She started to cry and Mrs. Feather sent her to the office.

Main Idea and Details, pp. 17–23

Guided Practice: Stars and Stripes Forever, pp. 19–20

1. Circle: Today, the flag still has 13 stripes. But it has 50 stars: one for each state in the United States.
2. Circle: The red stands for courage. The white stands for hope. The blue stands for truth.
3. Each star represents a state and that each state is free.
4. The United States flag is one symbol of our country.

Independent Practice: The National Symbol, pp. 21–22

1. The bald eagle is the national symbol of the United States.
2. Circle: It was chosen because of its long life, great strength, and majestic look.

3. Circle: The bald eagle lives in high mountains and steep cliffs. It has unlimited choice of where it will fly.
4. Possible answer: The Great Seal shows an eagle with its wings spread. It is facing forward and has a shield with 13 red and white stripes on its chest. The eagle holds an olive branch in its right talon.

Graphic Organizer: What's the Idea? p. 23

Main Idea: The bald eagle is a national symbol for the United States of America.
Detail: The bald eagle was chosen because of its long life, great strength, and majestic look.
Detail: The bald eagle stands for freedom.
Detail: A bald eagle is featured on the Great Seal of the United States.

Plot, pp. 24–30
Guided Practice: What a Mess! pp. 26–27

1. He went into the living room and watched his favorite cartoon show.
2. Circle: Next he got out the milk.
3. Underline: But the milk came pouring out. Before he knew it, the whole carton had emptied on the floor.
4. Marc used paper towels to wipe up the mess.
5. Underline: She said it was okay and helped him clean up the mess.
6. They went to get a breakfast treat and more milk.

Independent Practice: Going to the State Fair, pp. 28–29

1. Teva and her mom prepare to go to the state fair.
2. The car won't start.
3. Teva becomes upset when she realizes they won't make it to the fair.
4. Grandpa arrives.
5. Grandpa takes Teva and Mom to the state fair.

Graphic Organizer: Describe the Plot, p. 30

1. First: Mom and Teva get in their car to go to the state fair.
2. Then: Mom turns on the ignition, but the car doesn't start.
3. So: Mom says she'll call for a tow truck while Teva puts the snacks away.
4. Next: Teva hears a car honking. She runs outside and discovers that Grandpa is there with his truck.
5. After: Grandpa takes Mom and Teva to the state fair.
6. Last: While at the fair, the three family members go on rides, eat popcorn, and pet the animals.

Problem and Resolution, pp. 31–37
Guided Practice: It's Gone, pp. 33–34

1. Underline: Lalya

2. She can't find her homework.
3. She searches in the bedroom, kitchen, and every nook and cranny for her homework.
4. Circle: She thought about going to school without her homework.
5. She didn't think that was a good idea because doing her homework was something important to do.
6. Lalya redid her homework.

Independent Practice: Good Deed, pp. 35–36

1. B
2. C
3. A

Graphic Organizer: Problem and Solution, p. 37

Possible answer:

Main Character: Alonso
Problem: Alonso couldn't put the chicken and water in his mother's good china bowls.
Resolution: Alonso found two tubs and filled one with chicken and the other with water.

Prefixes and Suffixes, pp. 38–44
Guided Practice: Unpacking After a Camping Trip, pp. 40–41

1. Underline: *unpacking, unload*

2. Circle: *quickly, slowly, silently*
   Unpacking means the process of taking out things from a box that were already packed.
   Unload means to remove things such as boxes, that were stacked.
3. Underline: *unhook, untie, uncovered, unorganized;* Possible answer: Jorge keeps his homework unorganized in his backpack.
4. *unroll, unzip*
5. Circle: *smelled, finished*

Independent Practice: A Terrible Dream, pp. 42–43

1. A
2. C
3. A
4. B

Graphic Organizer: Words with Prefixes and Suffixes, p. 44

Possible answers:

Prefixes:

unable/"not able"

unusual/"not usual"

retell/"to tell again"

Suffixes:

scariest/"the most scary or frightening"

restless/"without rest"

useless/"not useful"

Author's Purpose, pp. 45–51

Guided Practice: Your Eating Habits, p. 47

1. The author wants us to know that eating healthy food is important to keeping us healthy.
2. to inform; The author wrote facts about healthy eating habits.

Guided Practice: Park or Mini-mall: You Decide, p. 48

1. The author likes the park. He/she says that people are happy to be at the park.
2. Underline: But we don't need more stores. We need our park.
3. to persuade

Independent Practice: The Letter, pp. 49–50

1. C
2. B
3. A

Graphic Organizer: Identify Author's Purpose, p. 51

Author's Purpose: to persuade

Evidence: drivers in the cars do not pay attention to the crossing guard; someone might get hurt; installing a stoplight will make getting to school safer

Setting, pp. 52–58

Guided Practice: A Hike to Remember, pp. 54–55

1. Circle: "in the mountains around our house"
2. Underline: "It was a Saturday morning. It was a beautiful spring day."

3. Underline: Possible answer: "I could hear a rumbling sound that was growing louder"; "Sounded like a small landslide"; "Rocks had fallen down the side of the rock wall. They had completely blocked the trail."

4. Possible answer: The landslide could only happen in the mountain setting.

Independent Practice: A Night Show, pp. 56–57

1. at night, after dinner

2. in the kitchen; outside in Oscar's backyard

3. Oscar and his parents clean up after dinner. Then they go outside to look at the stars.

4. Possible answer: The setting has to be at night and outside or the family could not look at the stars.

Graphic Organizer: Setting the Stage, p. 58

Where: Oscar's kitchen and backyard
When: a chilly evening in March